# 30-DAY CHALLENGE

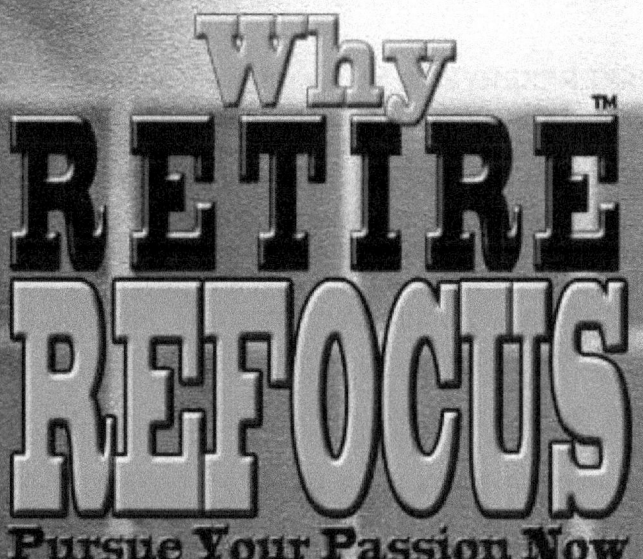

Lynn & Richard Voigt

# WHY RETIRE - REFOCUS
## Pursue Your Passion Now - 30-Day Challenge

© 2017 by RIVO Inc – All Rights Reserved!

ISBN-13: 978-1-940961-49-1
ISBN-10: 1940961-49-1

Cover Design & Interior Layout – RIVO Studios

**ALL RIGHTS RESERVED.** No part of this book may be reproduced or transmitted in any form whatsoever, known or yet invented, electronic or mechanical, scanning or photocopying, nor through any informational archival, storage, or retrieval system without prior written, dated, signed authorization of rights from RIVO Inc on behalf of the authors. All visual marks, images, and compositions included in this report, either in whole or in part, are governed and protected under International copyright and trademark laws by their rightful owner.

First Printing, 2017

Printed in the United States of America


## Visit Our Websites:

### www.RIVObooks.com
### www.WisconsinGarden.com

## Income Disclaimer

This book contains educational materials meant to inspire ways to promote personal ideas, products and services that may be appropriate to incorporate or use as a business strategy, marketing method or any other related personal or business idea that, regardless of the author's results and experience, may not produce the same results (or any results) for you. The authors make absolutely no guarantee, expressed or implied, that by using or following any of the ideas below that you will make money or improve current profits, as there are several factors and variables that come into play regarding any level of achievement or success in said personal matters and/or business venture. Primarily, results will depend on the nature of your efforts, your product or business model, the conditions of the marketplace, the experience of the individual, and situations and elements that are beyond your control.

As with any business endeavor, you assume all the risk related to investment and money based on your own discretion and at your own potential expense. If you intend to quote, copy, or use any content herein, in part or whole, it shall be the sole responsibility of you the individual to be mindful of all active and lawfully protected copyrights, trademarks, and/or services-marks, by conducting due diligence prior to said usage.

## Liability Disclaimer

This book is strictly intended for educational purposes only and was intended to inspire the individual to create ideas of their own design. This book represents the views of the authors as of the date of publication. Due to constant changing conditions facing the information age, the authors reserve the irrevocable right to modify and update their opinions based upon changing conditions. While the authors have made a "good faith" effort to verify the accuracy of information within this book, the authors or their affiliates/partners do not assume any liability or responsibility for inadvertent errors, omissions, or inaccuracies. This book is not intended to be used as a legal guide or resource, nor are the authors attempting to render any legal, accounting, or other said professional services. If legal consultation or advice is required, the authors recommend the reader immediately seek the services of a competent professional for all legal or accounting advice. It shall be the reader's responsibility to be fully aware of federal, state, local or country laws that govern and affect said business transactions. Any slight of ethnicity, culture, gender, orientation, or existing organization as is any reference to persons or businesses, living or dead, is unintentional and purely coincidental.

## Terms of Use

You are given a non-transferable, "personal use" license to read and use this book as desired. Also, there are no resale rights or private label rights granted when purchasing this book. In other words, it's for your own personal use only. Now that we clarified all of the legal stuff, let's begin to have a lifetime of fun by applying, modifying, and customizing the following educational materials to help you creatively live life productively, promote your own original ideas or develop your own marketing niche. Now that the legal mumbo-jumbo is out of the way, it's time for you to begin enjoying the fruits of our labor.

# GREATNESS COMES From Living With PURPOSE & PASSION

Ralph Marston

# WHY RETIRE - REFOCUS™

**30-Day Living With A Purpose Challenge**

I guess the real question you need to ask is "What Are Your True Intentions Now That You Say You Retired? As Kristin Armstrong once stated, *"We either Live with Intention or exist by default."* So what exactly are you retiring toward, and what is it that your truly want out of life?

Perhaps you've ended an illustrious 30, 40 or 50 year career and still have little or no clue as to what to do with all of your new free time.

This 30-Day challenge it's more than just learning more about living with purpose and work through the process of figuring out how to do just that over the course of 30 days. Here's a quick overview of the topics that can challenge your core belief system that establishes your priorities, daily opportunities and most importantly, your actions.

Here's What This 30-Day Challenge Offers:
1. What Does It Mean To Live With Purpose
2. Why It's Important To Find Your Purpose
3. What Is Your Purpose?
4. The Connection Between Purpose and Happiness
5. Why What You Do For A Living Matters
6. How To Find Your Calling
7. Your Purpose Doesn't Have To Be Huge To Make A Difference
8. Small Things You Can Do Right Now That Make A Difference
9. Do You Know What's Sucking Up Your Time
10. Going From Existing To Truly Living Life
11. Let's Talk About TV And The Likes
12. How Much Time Are You Spending On Facebook
13. Embrace Your Hobbies And Interests
14. Never Stop Learning
15. The Big Benefits Of Traveling The World
16. Creating Purposeful And Meaningful Relationships
17. When You Have Purpose, You Take Action Without Fear Of Failure
18. Living With Purpose Is Good For Your Spiritual Health
19. Guess What? Money And "Stuff" Doesn't Make You Happy
20. Living With Purpose Makes You A Kinder Person
21. When You Live With Purpose, You Don't Have Time To Worry
22. When You Live A Purpose Driven Life, Your Values Are Clear
23. You Realize The World Doesn't Revolve Around You
24. Aligning Yourself With Your Purpose Through Mediation And Prayer
25. Avoid Temptations And Wrong Paths Along The Way
26. Living With Purpose Is About Serving Your Community
27. Your Loved Ones Will Benefit From A Purpose Driven Life
28. Your Purpose May Evolve And Change As You Do… And That's Ok
29. What Do You Want To Be Remembered For?
30. Wrap Up And Where To Go From Here

## Day 1 - What Does It Mean To Live With Purpose

*"Life isn't about finding yourself. Life is about creating yourself."*
George Bernard Shaw

We've been thinking about the idea of living with purpose for quite some time. It's an interesting concept and something that can have a positive impact on your entire life. When we live with purpose, we get more done, we create meaning in our life, and most importantly, we feel happier and more fulfilled. That's why it's an important topic to discuss. It's also what inspired us to create a 30-day series of daily lessons around it.

Over the course of the month, we'll take a look at living with purpose and how we can start to live more intentionally. We'll look at how this will affect all aspects of our lives and of course, I will have plenty of hands-on tips and suggestions for you.

Let's start today by talking a little bit about what it means to live with purpose. In essence it means that you know what you're doing. You have goals and are passionate about what you do. Instead of simply letting the days pass you by, you work with purpose to make the most from each day.

Living with a purpose has a couple of big advantages over simply existing. When you know exactly what you want to do with your life, you have a clear plan or path. You don't have to get up each morning and then try to figure out what you will do. You simply jump in and keep working towards the goals you set based on your purpose.

You have a clear set of core values that you follow, based on your purpose. This will come in handy anytime you have a decision to make. Think of these values as your compass that keeps you on track.

Most importantly, living with purpose gives you a great sense of self-worth. You know what you're doing and you're actively working towards the goals you've set yourself. Not only does this increase your feeling of self-worth and self-confidence, living a purpose driven and fulfilled life will also greatly increase your overall happiness.

In the end, that's what it's really about, isn't it? We all want to live a happy and fulfilled life with meaning. That's why it's important to start thinking about living with purpose.

Last but not least, we'd like you to begin keeping a daily journal about your daily journey, self-image, problem-solving, clarifying want you want out of life, recording fresh thoughts, ideas and inspiration, and ultimately taking actions that will allow you to pursue your passion now, today! If you seek a unique daily journal, we offer them at www.RIVObooks.com.

## Day 2 - Why It's Important To Find Your Purpose

In yesterday's blog post we talked about what it means to live with purpose and I briefly touched on why it is important to do so. Today, I want to dive a little deeper and talk more about it. Making the decision to live your life with purpose, and then finding said purpose can have a profound effect on your life.

It Gives Your Life Meaning
When you decide on your life's purpose, it gives what you do a lot of meaning. Every step along the way, and all the work you do towards reaching your goals, serves to bring you one step closer. It becomes much easier to get things done, when they are done with purpose and with a firm goal in mind.

It Creates A Value System
Living with purpose also helps you define and set a system of core values that will guide you throughout the coming years. You don't have to waste time and energy each day trying to figure out if what you're doing is right or worth doing. As long as it aligns with your purpose, you know you're on the right track. That gives you a lot of confidence in what you are doing.

It Increases Your Feeling Of Self Worth
When you are living with purpose and working towards a worthwhile goal, you take a lot of pride in what you do. With each passing day, and each small step that you reach towards that goal, your sense of self-worth will also increase. Use that feeling to propel you through the next day and the next challenges ahead.

It Leads To Fulfillment and Happiness
Living a life with purpose, that's meaningful and gives you a sense of self-worth and confidence leads to happiness. Give it a try during this 30 Day Challenge and create a purpose for yourself. At the end of the month you'll notice that you are not only more confident, but also more fulfilled. The true secret to a happy life is being completely fulfilled by the life you're living.

We are social creatures who need to make a difference and have a purpose, a place in society. We may think that material things bring us happiness, but what truly matters is how meaningful, helpful, and purposeful what we do is. Don't be surprised to notice a measurable increase in your overall happiness at the end of this month-long challenge or journey towards a purpose driven life.

It's Good For Your Mental And Physical Health
Last but not least, living with purpose is good for your health. Being needed, being helpful, and adding value to the lives of others has a measurable effect on both your physical and mental health. Living a

purposeful life decreases your risk of heart disease and stroke, while it is also protecting you against depression. In fact, one of the best ways to fight depression is to find meaning and purpose in what you do each and every day.

## Day 3 - What Is Your Purpose?

The first step on this journey towards living with a purpose is deciding that it is a worthwhile endeavor. I hope the first two blog posts in this series have convinced you of that. The next step is to figure out what exactly your purpose in life is. It's a pretty big question, isn't it? I wish I had just the right answer for you, but the truth is that our life's purpose is different for all of us. There is no quiz you can take that spits out the answer. It's something you have to discover for yourself. I do however have a few thoughts to share with you that will guide you along the way. In the end, your purpose is very much like true love. You will know it when you've found it.

What Are You Passionate About?
Start by thinking about all the different things you are passionate about. It doesn't matter if it's part of your current work or career, a cause, a hobby, or anything else you can think of. Make a list and keep adding to it as you come across more ideas. Maybe it's restoring old cars, redecorating your home, or sewing historical costumes.

What Do You Value?
Another good approach for coming up with potential "purpose" ideas is to think about what you really value. What's important to you? What do you feel would make a difference? Maybe you value the right of every child to grow up in a happy home and make it your life's purpose to raise foster kids or adopt. Maybe you value animal rights and make it your mission to raise awareness about the low number of wild giraffes in Africa.

What Elicits A Strong Emotional Response?
Similarly, think about what makes you really happy, really angry, or really sad. Having something with a strong emotion attached is a good sign that you're very passionate about it and that this particular cause or purpose is important to you. Maybe it's passion on your love of playing piano, your passion for heirloom tomato gardening, or your burning desire to put a stop to human trafficking.

What's Fun
Last but not least, think about what you enjoy doing. There's nothing wrong with finding a purpose that is also enjoyable. In fact, it's important that you like what you do and are having fun doing it. If it isn't fun, it's much harder to put in the work and effort required to reach your goals.
Of course not every task and every aspect of what you do will be fun. Overall though, you want to find a purpose and a project that has you excited to jump out of bed in the morning.

## Day 4 - The Connection Between Purpose and Happiness

When we start to make a difference and live a purpose driven life, something amazing happens. We become happier and more fulfilled. I'm sure you've experienced this. It doesn't have to be anything big like going on a year-long mission trip or setting out to cure the world of cancer. Even small gestures that make a difference can have a big impact on how you feel.

When you help a fellow student pick up a stack of dropped books, run an errand for an elderly neighbor, loan a great book that's had an impact on your own life to a friend, or remind a fellow grocery shopper of a left bag, it feels good doesn't it? We like to help out and make a difference. It doesn't matter how small the act is.

We have been social creatures who rely on each other for millennia. Over the course of that time our bodies and brains have evolved to give us positive rewards for helping out and making a difference. In other words, it feels good to live with purpose and make a difference. It makes us happy.

It's one of the biggest reasons why living with purpose is such an important goal. At the end of the day, we all just want to be happy, or at the very least happier than we are right now. Looking at popular media and advertising in particular, it seems that the key to happiness is more material goods. We're made to believe that bigger and more expensive houses and cars, more clothes, shoes, furniture, electronics, workout gear and the likes are what will makes us happy. If only we can buy and accumulate enough "stuff", we'll feel better. Sadly, quite the opposite is true. The more you own, the more you have to worry about and take care of, taking away valuable time that you could be spending on something else.

The key to happiness isn't to own more. It's to live a purpose driven life and making a difference in the world. It's one of the reasons why minimalism is becoming so popular. When your life and mind isn't cluttered with all the extra stuff, you feel calmer, more in control, and have the time and mental energy to figure out your own purpose.

A purpose driven life is one lived within our core values. It caters to our need to cooperate and work together. It strengthens our confidence and makes us feel needed and valuable. All of this leads to an increased feeling of happiness. The moral of the story is stop buying stuff you don't need, stop chasing that high-paying job that makes you miserable for 60 hours a week and start living your life with purpose.

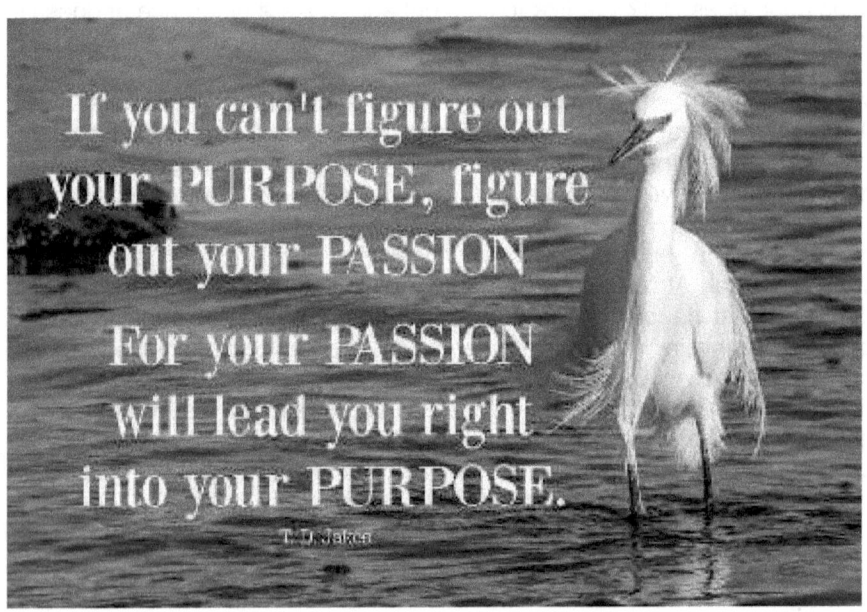

## Day 5 - Why What You Do For A Living Matters

What do you do for a living? That's a pretty big question, isn't it? Our job, our career, and how we earn money to finance our life is a big part of how we define ourselves. It's often one of the first pieces of information we share after our name when we meet someone else. It's a big part of our identity and of our feeling of self-worth.

We also spend a lot of time "on the job". Between the 40+ hours we actually spent at work, lunch breaks, commutes back and forth, and of course getting ready for or unwinding from work, this takes up most of our working hours. With this much time devoted to our job, doesn't it make sense to do something we enjoy and that brings us happiness?

This is why it matters what you do for a living. You're spending a lot of time training for your job, on your job, and thinking about your job. While not everyone will end up following their passion and working in a job that fulfills their purpose in life, it is something to keep in mind when you're getting ready to go into the workforce or are switching jobs. Sometimes, a change can be a very good thing.

On the flip side, we need to have a job that pays the bills so we can support our families. If you're a single mom, you may consider your purpose to be to spend as much time as possible raising your kids. Your dream job may be stay at home mom, but with no second parent to support your little family, that may not be possible. This is when it's time to look outside the box. Maybe you can find a way to work from home, or bring your kids to work with you. Maybe you can work two long overnight shifts as a nurse on the weekend while someone watches the kids and be there for them the rest of the week. There are ways to make your job work around your purpose, no matter what it may be.

Keep in mind that things don't have to be perfect. In fact, they seldom are. Perfection is not the goal. Leading a happy and fulfilled life is. Think about your current job. Does it work for you? What works well, and what doesn't? What small changes or tweaks can you make to improve what you've got? In other words, think about how you can change how you make a living to align with your purpose in life. Then make a plan to implement those changes.

## Day 6 - How To Find Your Calling

Finding and following your calling is a big part of living with purpose. Finding your calling can be an intimidating task, particularly if you put yourself under peer-pressure to immediately come up with the perfect answer. While it may be a goal worth pursuing, it's also important to realize that it may take time to find your true calling, which is a process that develops over time, and a calling that you cannot force. In fact, you shouldn't. A much better plan of action is to take it one step and one day at a time until your calling becomes crystal clear.

Start With What's Important To You
A great place to start is to think about what's important to you. It doesn't have to be huge or all-consuming. Start with something small. Find a cause you feel drawn to and do what you can to support it. Volunteer, learn more about it and share what you're learning with others, support organizations financially. Maybe this means knitting baby hats for preemies at your local hospital. Maybe it means spending time with an elderly neighbor, or maybe it means saving up for a mission trip next summer. The most important thing is to simply start and do something.

Listen To The Soft Voice In Your Head
Another great strategy is to listen to your intuition. Pay attention to that small voice in your head that tells you what you should be doing. Learning to listen to this little voice can be a bit of a challenge in today's busy and noisy world.

Spend some time contemplating your values. Educate yourself about causes that catch your attention. Spend some quite time in meditation or prayer to be able to hear the voice in your head. Then start taking action on what you're hearing and what you know you should be doing.

Walk The Path Towards Your Calling One Step At A Time
Don't let this process overwhelm you. In the first excitement, you may be tempted to tackle a huge project and set out to change the world all at once. While that's a great ambition, it's also something that can seem quite daunting and burn you out. Instead, take it one step at a time. Pick your path and get in the habit of doing something every week, or even daily that aligns with your calling and helps you reach your goals. Pick something that's easy to do and fit into your already busy life. No matter how small, every little act and effort helps to make a difference and serve with purpose.

**Day 7 - Your Purpose Doesn't Have To Be Huge To Make A Difference**
When we think about finding our calling or our life's purpose, it's easy to get caught up in these huge visions. We think that it has to be something along the lines of what Gandhi or Mother Teresa accomplished in their lifetimes. If you think that your purpose has to be this all-encompassing lifelong body of work, it's easy to get discouraged and never get off to a start in the first place. And no wonder... that type of "goal" is overwhelming and seems unattainable.

The good news is that you don't have to dedicate your entire life to your calling. It doesn't have to be this all-consuming thing. You can make a real difference on a small scale that will help those around you and give you the benefits of living a purpose driven life. Keep that in mind as you go on this journey of discovering, and fine-tuning your purpose and then living a purpose-driven life.

Let me share a few simple little examples with you of things that can be done with purpose that make a real difference to the people it touches. None of these is a huge project, none takes a lot of time or money, but they all have a noticeable impact, particularly over time. More important than finding a huge purpose or calling is to live your life going forward with purpose and intention.

### Spending Quality Time With Your Spouse And Kids

Our lives are hectic and busy. Often we don't spend any quality time with our loved ones. Instead we race from commitment to commitment, cramming in a few meals and a bit of parenting here and there before collapsing on the couch and mindlessly watching TV. Become more intentional and purposeful in how you spend time with your family. Set aside pockets of time each day to give them your full attention. Plan some fun outings and activities and truly reconnect with the people who are most important to you.

### Creating And Sharing Care Packages For The Homeless

Grab some gallon-sized Ziploc bags, head to the dollar store and put together small care packages for the homeless. Include a few personal hygiene products, some nonperishable food, and maybe a pair of socks or a hat. Keep them in your car and hand them out to homeless people you come across.

### Adopt A Soldier

Make the day of a soldier overseas with a monthly letter and small care package. Google "adopt a soldier" to learn more and to find a soldier or unit you can connect with.

### De-Cluttering Your Home And Downsizing Your Possessions

Let's bring it back home for this last example. Living with purpose is all about living intentionally. Why not declutter your home and downsize your possessions in general to make sure you have time, space, and finances to do so. Donate what you don't need any longer and see how much more free you feel when you're no longer weight down by all this extra "stuff".

Notice that living a purpose driven life doesn't always mean going out in the community and improving the lives of others. Another aspect that's just as important (and should in fact come first) of living with purpose is to do so when it comes to your personal life and your home. Start there and then branch out toward the world at large.

## Day 8 - Small Things You Can Do Right Now That Make A Difference

In yesterday's post we started to take a look at what you can do to live with purpose without getting overwhelmed by tackling too much at once. Today I thought I'd share a list of various things you can do to live more purposely and make a difference. Browse through the list below and use it as inspiration for things you can do. Try what seems interesting or fun or use it as a starting point to come up with your own ideas. Most importantly come up with a couple of small things and commit to doing them this week. It's time to start living with purpose now.

### At Home and At Work

Let's start with a couple of meaningful and purposeful things you can do around your house and office:

- Organize your desk.
- Learn a new language or skill.
- Pick up a new hobby.
- Reconnect with old friends.
- Write Thank You notes.
- Plan a romantic dinner.
- Plant a garden.
- Cook from scratch.
- Create a household budget.
- Take a continued education class.
- Go back to college.

### In Your Local Community

Another great place to look at when it comes to living with purpose is your local community. What activities can you participate in, and what can you do to help out. Here are a few ideas to get you thinking about this:

- Help out an elderly neighbor.
- Trade babysitting services with a friend.
- Attend and help out at a local church.
- Support local charities.
- Run a charity race.
- Help out at your child's school.
- Volunteer at a local animal shelter or soup kitchen.
- Donate to a local food pantry.

### In The World

Last but not least, there's a lot you can do to make a difference in the world at large. Some of it will require travel and thus a bit more planning (not to mention money), but there's also quite a bit you can do from home, thanks to the internet and our global connections. Here are a couple of ideas for you:

- Join and support charitable organizations.
- Learn about different cultures and languages.

- Support mission trips from your local community.
- Go on a mission trip.
- Travel and explore different cultures.
- Provide financial support to your favorite causes.
- Become active on social media to raise awareness.

I hope these ideas have inspired you to come up with your very own short list of simple things you can start doing right now to live with more purpose. Find one or two of them and start implementing them right away. Then keep coming back to your list for inspiration and to add to it as we go through the rest of this 30 day challenge.

## Day 9 - Do You Know What's Sucking Up Your Time

We live in hectic times and our most precious commodity is and always will be time. You can't grow more of it and when it's gone you can't get it back.

How often do you tell yourself that you can't do what you want to do because you don't have the time? We all do it. We want to live with more purpose, volunteer, or simply spend more quality time with our family and friends, but there just isn't enough time to do it.

The cold hard truth is that there is plenty of time. It's simply a matter of prioritizing what you spend it on and cutting out some of the things that suck up your time. We all have them and while the specifics may be different from person to person, the solution is the same for everyone. Find out where you spend your time and then make educated decisions on what's important and what isn't.

One of the best tools for figuring out exactly where you're spending your time is a time journal.

This can be a simple little notebook, a stack of scrap paper, an Evernote doc on your phone, or a spreadsheet on your computer. Next start writing done what you're doing every 15 minutes from the time you get up to the time you go to sleep. Keep this up for about a week and see what you come up with. Reviewing your time log can be an eye opening experience.

You may discover that you spent a lot more time on the computer doing busy work, or surfing the web than you realize. Or maybe you had no idea that you spent an average of four hours a night watching TV, or 2 hours per day commuting to and from work. In other words, you'll start to recognize patterns of behavior and where you tend to spend your time. While there are quite a few areas that we don't have a lot of control over (you have to show up for work or school, make time for personal hygiene, and get some sleep), there are quite a few hours in each day that we can fill however we like.

Keeping a time log for a week or two provides you with the information you need to be able to make educated and conscious choices about how to spend that time. That in turn allows you to live more purposefully, no matter what your goals and aspirations are. Sometimes, you want to sleep in, spend the day reading or playing video games, or simply daydream and that's ok. It's a great way to unwind, distress, and recharge. On other days, you may choose do so something more active or social. The point is that when you become aware of how and where you're spending your time, you have more control and can be more intentional with how you spent it.

**Day 10 - Going From Existing To Truly Living Life**
We all get stuck in a rut sometimes. We go through the motions, and have the days roll by without much fun or excitement. We are doing what we're supposed to be doing without questioning things or changing them up. We're all guilty of this at some point or another. We get into a comfortable routine and are afraid to step outside of our comfort zone and try something new. While that may be a safe and secure way to live life, we end up spending our time merely existing instead of truly living life to the fullest.

The key to moving from letting the days pass you by to creating a meaningful life that you'll look back on with pride is intention and purpose. That's it. You simply have to step in, take control, and figure out what you want your life to be. Sounds pretty easy, doesn't it?

Of course that's easier said than done. If it wasn't, there would be no reason to run this 30 day challenge, and there wouldn't be bestselling books written on the topic. The biggest problem is that we're all very good at coming up with excuses about why we can't do what we actually would like to do. We come up with the excuses because they keep us safe. They keep us from trying new things and taking risks. They keep us from having to deal with possible disappointment.
There are things you want to do in life but maybe you're too shy or embarrassed because you're overweight or your hair is red or you have pimples or...the list goes on and on. I'm sure you have one of these that's a mile long.

The difference between existing and living is in the DOING! Who cares if you're a little out of shape and overweight? Who cares if you're doing something by yourself because you don't have a group of friends interested in the same things you are. Who cares if everyone around you has an opinion about what you're doing. Do it anyway.

Learn to feel good about yourself, gain some confidence, love yourself, and just do the things you love. Start truly living your life to the fullest instead of simply existing. Trust me, it is well worth the risk. One way to get over the fear of the unknown and step out of your comfort zone is asking yourself "What's the worst that could happen?" Often the worst scenario you can possibly imagine isn't nearly as scary as the unknown.

That one little exercise may just do the trick to convince you to give the things you've always wanted to do a try. I challenge you to pick one thing, one activity, just something and do it this week. Do it today if you can. Take action and take charge of your life and your purpose.

## Day 11 - Let's Talk About Television And The Likes

Here's a scary question for you. How much time do you spend each week sitting mindlessly in front of the TV, surfing the internet, playing video games and such? If you're anything like the average American it's a lot more than you'd like to admit or even think possible.

Don't get me wrong. It's fun to sit down and watch your favorite TV show or hang out and game. When it's intentional and this is how you choose to spend your time, go for it and enjoy. It only becomes problematic when time flies by and before you know it is three hours later and you have no idea what just happened. That's when TVs, gaming consoles, laptops, tablets and the likes become time suckers.

Why is this a problem? Because time is the only truly limited resource we're working with. If push comes to shove, you can find a way to get more of everything else, be it money, friends, or something easy like bread. But time, we can't get back and we don't get more of. There's no way to earn a few extra hours. We all work with 24 of them per day. Since they are our most limited resource, we should make sure we use them wisely and intentionally.

Today's challenge for you is to simply become more aware of what's sucking up a lot of your time when it comes to this type of entertainment. Instead of mindlessly popping down on the couch after a day at work and drifting off until it's time to go to bed, think about it before you do. Is this how you want to spend your time? If so, go ahead. If there's something else you want to try, go for it. In other words start making conscious choices about your free time.

Maybe you decide to go for a walk first, or meet up with a friend for a couple of beers before heading to the living room. Maybe you decide to read a book or have a meaningful conversation with your spouse or children. Maybe you decide to dust off the old board games for some old-fashioned interactive family fun. Pick what makes the most sense to you. Find something purposeful to do with all those extra hours in your day.

You'll be amazed at just how much free time you have once you stop wasting it away. Suddenly there is time for that new hobby you thought you couldn't get around to. There's time to work in exercise and still find time to watch your favorite movie. Being intentional and purposeful with your time, particularly during those times of the day when it would otherwise slip through your hands can have a profound on your life and your wellbeing.

## Day 12 - How Much Time Are You Spending On Facebook

In yesterday's blog post we talked about the time we spend vegging out in front of the TV or computer and how that time slips away from us. Today, I want to tackle another big time thief – social media. Don't get me wrong, it's an amazing tool, but it can also be quite distracting. It doesn't matter if it's Facebook, Pinterest, Tumbler, Instagram, or your social media platform of choice.

The biggest problem with social media is that it's everywhere. We check in from our computers, tablet, and of course the ever-present smart phone. We get alerts, we check in when we're bored, or have a couple of minutes to kill. Before we know it, thirty minutes or more have gone by that we're not getting back.

Here's an eye-opening exercise for you. Carry a pen and paper around with you, get a click counter or an app on your phone and start keeping track of how many times you access social media per day. Include any and all devices you use and add to the running total even when you're just looking at it "for a second". If you're anything like me, you'll be a bit shocked by how high that number actually is. This is one distraction that isn't usually caught by the time log we talked about a few days ago since the social media interactions are so quick and frequent. Trust me though, no matter how briefly you access each platform, it all starts to add up and distracts you from other things.

How often do you miss part of a conversation or a fun moment with your kids because you were busy commenting on a Facebook post, retweeting something, or pinning a fun craft idea that you likely won't get around to trying? Is it worth missing all those important little moments in life? And think about what you would have time and mental energy to do if you weren't constantly distracted by social media?

The goal is to live more intentionally and do things with purpose. We don't want to let social media posts distract us from that goal. I'm not saying that there isn't a time to use social media, far from it. They are a wonderful tool and a great way to connect with people. But they are also dangerously addictive. Don't believe me?

Here's another exercise for you. Commit to not using social media at all for 48 hours. Turn off or ignore the alerts on your phone and don't allow yourself to go to the sites on your computer. How does that feel? Do you miss it? Does it make you nervous or anxious?

It's time to take control over social media instead of letting it control us. What can you change starting today to make that happen?

**Day 13 - Embrace Your Hobbies And Interests**
Over the past few days we've taken a look at how we spend our time, what we spend it on and what may be sucking time away from us. In other words, we started to be more intentional on how we spend our time and what we spend it on. That leaves quite a few hours each week open to new things. When we're no longer watching TV mindlessly, or let social media suck us in, we have time to do the things we thought we simply didn't have time for.

Today I want to encourage you to embrace your hobbies and interests. Do you remember having all afternoon, weekends, and school holidays to do what you loved to do? Without the obligations of adulthood, it's easy to enjoy a hobby or explore other interests. When we become adults, it can become tougher to sneak in those activities between everything that has to be done. We often let go of the things we enjoy doing to the most. It's time to take back that joy and pick up those hobbies and interests again ...or even find something new to try.

Hobbies are an important part of living with purpose. They give balance to our lives and allow us to spend some much needed time on something we enjoy. They help us distress and are fun. For example, if you work in an office job where you spend most of your time working away at the computer all day, it can be tough to see the fruits of your labor. You work hard, but at the end of the day, you don't see anything in front of you that shows what you've accomplished. To balance this out, consider a hobby like gardening, sewing, knitting, or woodworking. Spend an hour in the evening on your favorite hobby and you can actually see, feel, and touch the progress you've made.

Hobbies can also help us unwind and let go of all the stress and anxiety that has built up over the workday. This in turn is good for our health and mental wellbeing. People with relaxing hobbies like playing music, crafting, painting, or gardening to name a few tend to sleep better and feel more refreshed when they can engage with their favorite past time.

Hobbies also give us a chance to connect with other likeminded individuals. There are classes, groups, clubs, and even guilds for all sorts of different things. Or you can simply form your own group. Find a few other cycling enthusiasts and start organizing group rides on the weekends. Start a monthly book club for a chance to discuss your favorite works of fiction with other readers. Embrace your hobbies and interests and make them part of your everyday life again.

## Day 14 - Never Stop Learning

As children, learning is an important part of our lives. We continue on as young adults through college and learning on the job. But then, by the time we hit our thirties, many of us stop learning on a regular basis. We may pick up something new here or there, or learn a new piece of software or equipment at work. But for the most part, we feel that we've acquired all the knowledge we need in life. While that's technically true, there is a lot to be said about lifelong learning.

Does this mean that you should go back to school as an adult? Not necessarily. While that's certainly an option, formal education in a school or university setting isn't the only way we learn and there's a lot of advantages to self-learning in a variety of ways. Lifelong learning keeps your mind strong, helps you stay up-to-date on technology in a fast paced and every changing world, and improves quality of life.

Independent or self-paced learning can take a lot of different forms. You might simply decide to read up on a particular course through a variety of google searches. You can teach yourself a new skill through online articles and YouTube videos. Listening to audio books or formal lectures like those available at the "Great Courses" website are another option. And of course there are plenty of online and local courses you can take on all sorts of topics. Take a workshop, learn a new language, or find a new hobby that requires new skills. There is an almost unlimited about of knowledge out there that you can learn.

Learning is wonderful because it keeps us curious and our mind active. There's a lot of pride and confidence that comes out of mastering a new skill, or figuring out a tough problem. Think of learning as a way to exercise your mind. Continued learning helps us understand the world around us, and the people in it better. That in turn will make us more compassionate and of course well-informed individuals. As an added bonus, self-paced learning is a great way to practice self-motivation, a skill that will come in handy throughout life.

Think about what you're doing already that is part of life-long learning. What are some things you would like to learn? Start making a short list of knowledge and skill goals and then start tackling them one a time. Maybe you've always wanted to learn how to knit, or you're interested in medieval history. Maybe you want to build your own computer, or learn how to operate a lathe. Make a plan and start making life-long learning a habit.

## Day 15 - The Big Benefits Of Traveling The World

Let's talk about something fun today – traveling the world or at least making an effort to travel more and further than you are now. Not only is it a lot of fun, it's also good for you and can help you live a more purpose driven life. Of course if one of your big goals is to travel more and see as much of the world as you can, this is a no-brainer. Even if traveling isn't one of your ambitions right now and you're perfectly comfortable staying in your little corner of the world, I encourage you to explore the option and give travel a try.

We live in a very global and interconnected world. Experiencing more of it in person will help you understand it better, which brings us to the first big benefit of traveling the world…

### Experience New Cultures

As you travel the world and interact with the people living there, you learn a lot about different cultures. It's fun to try new food, go shopping in a very different atmosphere and looking at very different products, stumble through conversations in a foreign language, and just soak up the fact that things can be done differently. Traveling is a great way to experience new cultures and learn from those experiences.

### Become More Open Minded

This in turn helps you become more open minded. You realize that there is more than one way to do things in all areas of life. Cooking is done differently, parenting is done differently, and even the rhythm of life might be very different. And that's just the beginning. You will come across all sorts of new ideas that challenge the way you've been thinking about things. That's a good thing because it gives you the opportunity to rethink how you're doing things and become more intentional and purposeful in what you do.

### Get Out Of Your Comfort Zone

Because so many things are done very differently and the entire culture is different from your own, traveling gets you out of your comfort zone. It's great when you feel like you're stuck in a rut or just need some fresh inspiration.

When we stay in our comfort zone, it's hard to grow and it's hard to change how we live our lives. Stepping out of that zone and doing things that are new, uncomfortable, and challenging is how we grow has human beings. Traveling is a great way to do that.

Even if traveling isn't big on your "to-do" list right now, I encourage you to make it a priority. If actual world travel isn't an option for you right now, do a bit of armchair traveling by learning more about a foreign country including its culture and language.

## Day 16 - Creating Purposeful And Meaningful Relationships

A big part of living a more intentional and purpose-driven life is the relationships we have. We are social creatures and we need other people around us to feel happy and complete. That means creating purposeful and meaningful relationships with family, friends, coworkers, and acquaintances.

While all relationships are important, the ones that will have the biggest impact on your own personal life are family and close friends. That's where you should start. These are the people that mean the most to you and often the ones you spend a lot of your time with. While good work relationships are also important, they don't have to be quite as deep and meaningful as personal relationship. As long as you communicate well with your coworkers and boss for example and you get along ok, you're good to go. With your best friend, your spouse, or your grandma on the other hand, working on a more meaningful relationship can have a huge impact.

Be Intentional In Your Relationships
The first step in having more meaningful relationships is taking a look at where you're at right now and then figuring out where you would like it to be. Do you want a more intimate relationship with your spouse? Do you want to be closer with your kids and have them open up to you? Do you want to have a more relaxed relationship with your book club friends? Once you know how you would like those relationships to be and look like you can work on being more purposeful and intentional in your interactions with those people.

Don't Like Something? Change It
Most relationships aren't perfect. Some are downright awful. While we can't change people, we can change our relationship with them. Sometimes that means setting boundaries. Sometimes, that may even mean cutting people out of our lives most of the time though, it means working on the relationship and having open and honest conversations. Work with the other person to come up with something that works well for both of you. Compromise and put in the effort to improve the relationship the two of you have for the better.

Good Relationships Take Work
Last but not least, I want you to realize that a good relationship takes work. This is true or your marriage, your relationship with your kids, staying close to your best friend and any other close relationship you can think of. If you get lazy and start taking it for granted, it will wither and die. Don't let that happen.

Instead, put in the work. Get up early in the morning to go for a run with your husband, spend the time to talk to your kids over dinner instead of popping down in front of the TV, and make the time to go hang out with your friends regularly. Be intentional about your relationships and do your part to make sure they stay meaningful and strong. Yes, it takes work, time, and effort, but it is well worth it.

**Day 17 - When You Have Purpose, You Take Action Without Fear Of Failure**

Something remarkable happens when you start to think about, and then live your life more purposefully. You start taking action. You start doing things instead of second guessing yourself and procrastinating. You get off the couch and get going on the things you've always wanted to do.

Taking action becomes so much easier when you have a clear purpose. You have a goal in mind and you know exactly what the next step is that you need to take. Even more importantly, you are highly motivated to get it done.

Let's look at weight loss as an example. You can try to lose some weight and get into shape for months and even years with little success. Sure, you eat a little better and you go for a walk every now and then, but because you don't have an actual purpose, you don't get far. You also occasionally give in to the urge to snack, get second helping, or indulge in a cookie. There's no big reason to get serious about losing weight and there's no deadline.

Now pretend you're getting married in nine months and you are determined to look great on your big day. You have a dress or suit size in mind and a pretty good idea of how many pounds you have to lose by your wedding day. Suddenly you have a purpose, a goal, and a deadline. That's exactly what it takes to get serious about losing weight.

You start taking massive action. You clean up your diet, cut out the sugar and processed food. You start working out to tone and reshape your body as you start to drop those pounds. You read up on and learn as much as you can about nutrition and the latest trends in diet and exercise. Best of all the pounds start to drop and you're looking better and better the closer you get to your non-negotiable deadline.

That's the power of having a purpose in action. It spurs you on and motivates you to do things and make changes. Having a purpose also keeps you from procrastinating out of a false fear of failure. Does that mean you won't fail? Of course not. There's a chance you may not hit your weight loss goal and there a very good chance that you'll cheat and have a doughnut or the likes at some point on your weight loss journey. That's not the point and not the type of failure I'm talking about.

No matter what because of your purpose you're going to make some serious progress and even if you stumble, you pick yourself up and get right back to it... because you have an important purpose that's motivating you. Not trying because you think you may fail is no longer an option and that's a pretty big deal.

## Day 18 - Living With Purpose Is Good For Your Spiritual Health

Today I want to talk about spiritual health or wellness and the affect living with purpose has on it. I don't care what your own spirituality or religion is. We live in a very diverse society and as a result, some of my readers will have different believes than others. Even within a group of people from the same faith or belief system, there are fast differences between individual faiths or spiritual beliefs. In the end, living with purpose and intention is beneficial, no matter what you belief.

Having a purpose is a primal human need. We want to be needed and we need to know that we're making a difference in order to feel fulfilled, happy, and complete. That's why living with purpose is so important and why it is good for your overall spiritual health.

The Need To Be Needed
We like to be needed by others. It makes us sad and lonely when we can't help those around us and make a difference in their lives. Having a purpose and living with purpose allows us to do just that on a regular basis. It fulfills the need to be needed.

The Need To Find Meaning In Life
Another common human desire or need is to find meaning in life. We don't like to feel like we're wasting our time here. Living with purpose gives meaning to each day. That in turn makes us feel happier and more fulfilled.

The Need To Have Hope
At the end of the day, even when things seem bad, we need to have hope. Having a purpose means we have a plan and we have something to strive towards. That's hope there. It is hope that we'll make a difference, it is hope that things will get better, and it is hope that we can get ourselves out of the hole we find ourselves in.

The Need For Values
We also need values to live a happy and fulfilled life. Our values are like a compass that guides us along the way. If you are a parent, you know how important it is to impart strong values on your children. Without them they feel lost and insecure. That can add a lot of stress and unhappiness. We're no different as adults. Living our life with purpose by default provides us with a strong set of values to live by.

Living with purpose is good for the mind and spirit. It allows you to live a more fulfilling and happier life and make a difference in the world.

**Day 19 - Guess What? Money And "Stuff" Doesn't Make You Happy**
In yesterday's blog post we talked about the importance of living with a purpose for your spiritual health and how it all comes back to living a happy and fulfilled life. Today I want to talk about what doesn't make you happy. We've talked a lot so far about why it's important to live with purpose, and a big part of it is because it makes you feel happier and more content.

What doesn't make you happy is money and more material possessions. In fact, quite the opposite seems to be true. Yes, of course there's a time when a little extra cash and a more reliable car increase you happiness and decrease your stress and worries. There's a threshold below which money and material possessions do make us happier. But once we reach a level where we live somewhat comfortably and don't have to worry about having food in the fridge and a roof over our head, something interesting happens.

From there on out, more money and more possessions simply gives us more "stuff" to worry about. In those cases an increase in material and monetary possessions doesn't increase happiness. The goal then shouldn't be to do everything we can to keep up with the Joneses. Instead, what makes us happy is living a purpose driven and meaningful life.

Deep down you already know this. Meaningful experiences trump material gifts anytime. We remember the fun trips we took as kids or the time we got to see a concert much more vividly than a pile of presents under the tree. Yes, there are exceptions like the year you got the new bike, but that's when there was purpose and meaning attached to the material gift.

The goal then, when we want to increase our overall happiness and wellbeing shouldn't be to accumulate as much money and stuff as possible. It should be to focus on having the basic needs covered so we don't have to worry too much, and then shift our focus to experiences and relationships. That's the true key to leading a happy and fulfilled life.

It also means focusing on finding purpose in what we do. Instead of, or better in addition to financial goals, start making ones for relationships, experiences, and the likes. Instead of focusing on that next big promotion or bonus check, or how you'll afford a new car, spend your time and energy on the things and people that are important for you.

Start living with purpose and start making a difference. That's what will increase your happiness and wellbeing along with that of those around you.

> There is no greater gift you can give or receive than to honor your calling. It's why you were born. And how you become most truly alive.
>
> Oprah Winfrey

## Day 20 - Living With Purpose Makes You A Kinder Person

When we're stressed out, working too hard, and running around to meet the latest deadline, or pay a stack of bills, we're often not the nicest people to be around... far from it. If on the other hand, we shift our focus and live our life with purpose and intention, this changes. Living with purpose makes us kinder and nicer. Why is that?

Living With Purpose Helps You Focus On Others
Living with purpose often includes other people. It's about those around you as much as about yourself. We are social creatures and we like to work with, interact with, and help those around us. When we make those relationships a priority, we take the needs of others into account. That teaches us empathy and understanding, which in turn makes us nicer and kinder to those around us.

Living With Purpose Takes You Out Of The Competitive Mindset
When we stop trying to keep up with the Joneses and compete for the highest paying job, biggest car, and nicest house, we stop competing with everyone around us. Life is about much more than outdoing everyone else. When we realize that and focus on relationships, experiences, and helping each other out, we are kinder because we're no longer competing for the number one spot.

Living With Purpose Reduces Stress
Since you're no longer participating in the rat race in the same way as before, and instead embrace meaningful activities and relationships that make you happier, it should come as no surprise that your level of stress is greatly reduced. I don't know about you, but I'm not the kindest person when I'm stressed out. When I'm more relaxed and fulfilled on the other hand, being kind is a natural state of mind.

Living With Purpose Increases Happiness
As we've already established in previous blog posts in this series, living a purpose driven life makes us happier. It shouldn't come as a big surprise to you that you're kinder and nicer to be around when you're in a good mood. It's when we're stressed out, or feeling trapped, mad and angry at the world that we aren't so much fun to be around.

To recap, living with purpose does quite a few things to make you a kinder, nicer person to be around. If that's not a great motivator to work towards a more purposeful life, I don't know what is.


## Day 21 - When You Live With Purpose, You Don't Have Time To Worry

Are you a worrier by nature? Do you spend your time worry about anything and everything that could go wrong? I've been there and done that. It's not the most pleasant or most productive use of your time. When we worry a lot, it tends to paralyze us. We're too worried about everything we don't know yet, what's out of our control and what could go wrong. As a result, we don't get to the important part of taking action, no matter what the goal or activity was.

When we embrace living with purpose the act of worrying changes dramatically. When you know exactly what you want and have the passion to go after it, everything becomes clear. You know what your first step is and then the next one after that. You get to work and start making progress. You keep going and keep working away to make sure you get done what you've set out to do. In the end, you simply don't have time to worry about all that small stuff and that's a very good thing.

Most worrying is frankly pointless. It uses up brain space and energy that would be much better spent other places. That doesn't help you much when you're busy worrying about anything and everything. What will help you is shifting your focus, your energy, and your passion to something more productive – your purpose.

When you find your purpose and make it an integral part of your life, you'll simply be too busy to worry. The cure to too much worrying then is taking massive action. Go do something that aligns with your purpose. It doesn't matter what it is. Start with something small that feels safe. Getting that task under your belt will show you that your worries were unfounded and that you can push through them. It also gives you a sense of accomplishment and that in turn builds confidence.

Confidence is another great weapon against the paralyzing effect of worrying. Confident people don't worry. With each action you take, you become a little more confident and a little less worried. Build on each success and keep working on your self-confidence.

Keep focusing on why the things you do are important to you and why you embraced a particular purpose. Focusing on how it is helpful to others is another great tool that will help you push through and start taking action. That in turn builds confidence and decreases worries. Before you know it, you too will be too busy to worry because you're taking action toward living a purpose driven life.

**Day 22 - When You Live A Purpose Driven Life, Your Values Are Clear**
Today, I want to talk about values. They guide our lives and are like a compass to keep us on the clear and narrow. We learned basic values as young children, and then continue to evolve and adapt them as we grow into adulthood. Along the way things can sometimes get murky. Part of growing up involves questioning the values we've grown up with and

sometimes, we simply disregard some of the values we've grown up with without setting up a clear new system of values

The beauty of living a purpose driven life is that as soon as you start paying attention to what you want to accomplish and start to live with purpose, your values become clear. You know without a shadow of a doubt what's most important to you. You may choose family over a big raise or overtime. You may choose working hard now and saving up over instant gratification. You may choose going out and making friends or exercising (or both at once) over sleeping in on the weekend. You get the idea.

When you live with purpose... no matter how big or small those purposes may be... you live based on values. When you look at it and think about it for a minute, those values will become very clear to you. You'll learn what's most important to you. That in turn will help throughout the rest of your life moving forward

Once you are clear about your values and have them defined, it becomes much easier to make daily decisions and choices. With your value compass in place, you only have to ask yourself if what you are doing is aligning with those values. That in turn makes your life a lot easier. You no longer have to agonize or second guess yourself. Instead, you make your decision and are confident that it's the right one.

Having a moral compass and set of values gives you a lot of confidence. You know, without a shadow of a doubt, that you're doing the right thing and are moving in the right direction. Between that and the passion and excitement a purpose driven life brings, you'll feel like you're on the right path. That takes a lot of stress, worry, and second guessing out of the equation, which is a very good thing.

You find yourself calmly moving through life, making decisions, taking action, and moving along almost effortlessly. I'm sure you've noticed people around you who have a strong purpose and values. They stride through life instead of stumbling. That's the goal and that's what I want you to get out of this 30 Day Living with Purpose challenge. Start paying attention to your own moral compass of values and let it guide you well on this sometimes complicated, and sometimes treacherous path of living life.

**Day 23 - You Realize The World Doesn't Revolve Around You**
Much of what's going on in today's world makes us focus on ourselves. We're supposed to look out for our best interest, compete with others for the best job, the biggest car, and the nicest house. We're surrounded by advertisements and media messages that encourage us to be very self-centered and ego-centrical.

When we start to live with purpose, the people around us become more important. Instead of focusing on just us, we focus on our family, our community, and even the world at large. That's quite a bit of a change in perspective and something that will come over time. The amazing thing is that it starts happening effortlessly.

You start by living more purposefully and end up focusing more on the needs of your loved ones. Maybe it starts with simply paying more attention to your spouse and kids. From there it moves toward your extended family and your circle of friends. Along the way you notice that working with others, helping them out, and doing things for them feels good and brings a lot of joy and happiness. Living a purpose driven life that includes other people who are important to us is a great feeling.

From there it spirals out. As you create more intentional relationships with your kids for example, you get closer to their friends. You also become more empathetic to the needs of other parents and their children. Your focus starts to shift from yourself and your own little family to your local community and eventually the global community we all live in. And that's a very good thing.

No matter how much it is drilled into us and how much we want to believe it, we don't live in a bubble. We live in a community and in this day and age that community reaches across the entire globe. Our actions, our purchases, and how we choose to live our lives has an impact on everyone else. We can no longer afford and shouldn't want to live a self-centered life. Trust me, being part of a community and working together for the better of everyone involved is a much better feeling.

It's yet another advantage to living your life with purpose. You get to see the world from a different perspective. Not only that, but you'll also be setting a good example for your children and other people around you. As they see you care about and help others, they will be inspired to do the same. If you ask me that's pretty powerful stuff. Your own choice to live with purpose can end up affecting hundreds, if not thousands of others and inspire them to do the same.

**Day 24 - Aligning Yourself With Your Purpose Thru Mediation And Prayer**
Living with purpose isn't always easy. We get busy, we get stressed out, or we simply get distracted. It happens to all of us and when it does, we no longer hear that little voice in our head clearly that tells us what we should be doing. Without a clear purpose and solid intentions to live our life around it, it becomes easy to get off course. We have to find a way to make sure we can get back on track and realign ourselves with the purpose we've chosen.

A great way to do this is through prayer and meditation. There's a reason these techniques have been used for millennia by spiritual leaders and everyday people who successfully live a purpose driven life. Both prayer and meditation allow you to tune out those distractions and give you clarity of mind. Once your mind quiets, you can start to listen to that inner voice that tells you what's truly important and what you value most.

It doesn't matter what religion you belong to, if you consider yourself a spiritual person, or how much faith you have. Prayer and meditation can benefit anyone. One of the easiest forms of meditation is a simple breathing exercise that you can do anytime, anywhere. That being said, I recommend you practice it first in a calm and quiet spot. This will allow you to focus on it and get used to it without too many distractions. Once you've practiced for a little while though, you can use it to calm and clear your mind whenever you need it.

A Simple Breathing Mediation
The easiest type of meditation is to simply focus on your breath. Try to tune out everything else and focus on breathing in and breathing out. Notice how the air feels flowing through your noise. Pay attention to how your abdomen rises and falls, expands and contracts. Whenever you get distracted or start to think of something else, keep bringing yourself back to the breath. Start by practicing it for 30 seconds to a minute and expand the time with practice.

Give this a try and see if you find it helpful. From there read up on other meditation techniques. There are lots of great books out there on the topic. There are guided meditations and even mobile apps.

## Day 25 - Avoid Temptations And Wrong Paths Along The Way
We've been talking about living with purpose for quite some time. By now you've thought quite a bit about what you may want to change or tweak in your own life to live more intentionally and with more purpose. Ideally you will have started to incorporate some of those ideas and are starting to live more purposefully.

Old habits are hard to break and it's not uncommon to slip back into familiar behavioral patterns that no longer align with your wish to live more intentionally. In addition there will be things and people tempting you to stray off you path as well. You may have the best of intentions to live healthier or example and take better care of your body, but when you walk into the break room at work there's a big box of doughnuts tempting you. Or maybe you are trying hard to be more patient and understanding with your young children on a day when they are determined to push all your buttons and test the limits of that new patience. It happens. Life is messy and there will always be things that go wrong and people who intentionally or unintentionally try to lead us down the wrong path.

The best way to deal with temptations is to expect them. They are going to show up sooner or later. If they surprise you, you will be more likely to give in. If you know they are coming, you can guard yourself better against them. Learn from each temptation and realize that each one you avoid makes you stronger and more determined to stay your course.

Even with the best intention and our guard up against temptation we can end up heading down the wrong path. Life happens and sometimes things are out of our control. At other times, we may not notice that we've chosen a wrong turn until we're well up that wrong path. It's ok. It happens. It's simply time to change course and get back on track. This is why it is importantly to frequently review what we're doing. This allows us to see what's happening and if what we're doing is still aligned with our intentions, our purposes, and our values. Make sure you take this time for reflection and adjust as needed as you go along on this exciting journey of living a purpose driven life.

## Day 26 - Living With Purpose Is About Serving Your Community

One of the most eye-opening experiences for me when I started to live with purpose was that life is about so much more than just me in my little bubble. Living a full and meaningful life means being part of a community and serving it in a variety of ways. Let's look at a few of them.

Your Inner Circle
The first community you encounter and the one you spent most of your time in is your very own inner circle. By living more purposefully and more intentional, you'll have the most influence on this one. It's your inner circle that's compromised of your family and close friends. These are the people you spent the most time with. It may also include your coworkers. This is the community you should focus on first. Start making a difference with the people you're closest too.

Your Local Community
Your next step will be your local community. It's amazing how much change you can affect here when you put your mind to it. Let's say you want to live a life where you're more aware of the impact you have on your environment. You shop smarter, recycle and reuse more at home. From there you can branch out into your local community and encourage positive change. Start a community garden and encourage people to recycle more. Get involved with communal policy that's focused on environmental efforts. Join the organizations that are already present within your own local community.

Finding Your Niche In The Global Community
One of the amazing things of being alive today is how connected we are. The internet, mass communication, and fast travel make it possible to

connect with people from all around the world. We all do it to some extent. Some of us work in global companies that get us in touch with team members who live in different countries or come from different cultures. We may connect with people online who enjoy the same hobby. We do more traveling today than ever before which of course exposes us to different ways of living and different cultures. We watch TV shows and movies from various different parts of the world. We have in fact become global community and that gives us a unique opportunity. As a result, living purposefully and taking part in online groups and global efforts can bring about change that affects the global community. That's pretty powerful, isn't it?

## Day 27 - Your Loved Ones Will Benefit From A Purpose Driven Life

In yesterdays' post we talked about how we can use our communities to have long lasting, permanent change by living a purpose driven life. Those changes can be small or large, and they all add up. We can make a difference. Today I want to take a look at the impact living a purpose driven life can have on your loved ones.

### You Set A Good Example

The most powerful thing about living your life with purpose is that you are setting a good example for those around you. Trust me, your kids are watching. Your spouse or significant other is noticing what you're doing. So are your family and friends. Living a purpose driven life can be quite contagious. Start and see how much of an effect you can have on those around you.

In other words, not only will they benefit from what you do directly (by being more attentive and patient for example, or making an effort to spend more quality time with people important to you), they also benefit by being encouraged to live a more purposeful life themselves.

### You're More Confident In Yourself

As you start to live with purpose and see the impact even small acts can have you're more confident in yourself. As you gain self-confident, you start to feel more comfortable in your skin. You're making a difference and live with purpose. This in turn makes you a more confident parent, spouse, and friend. Your loved ones will benefit because you are no longer busy second guessing yourself. You take massive action that benefits everyone.

### You're Happier And More Fulfilled

One of the big reasons self-confidence is so important is that it is directly linked with how happy you feel. Add to that the fact that living a life with purpose is very fulfilling and it's no wonder that you are happier and more content once you start living with purpose and intention.

All this in turn will make you a kinder and better person overall. Living a purpose driven life makes you a better parent, a better spouse, a better coworker and a better friend. It has a positive impact on all the people who are close to you and who have an important part in your life. Keep that in mind as you continue on this journey of living with purpose. Use it as motivation and encouragement on those days when things get hard and you're ready to give up. Don't let them or yourself down.

**Day 28 - Your Purpose May Evolve And Change As You Do… And That's OK**
I'm sure throughout this challenge you've been thinking a lot about living with purpose and what that means to you right now. Hopefully you're living more intentionally already and are changing things here and there to better align with your purpose. You may even discover your big passion and your calling and working towards making that happen. That's great, but there's something we haven't talked about much. It's that we all grow and change as time goes by. And with that our purposes change.

Let's say you're a mother of small children. Right now, living with purpose may mean to spend as much time as possible raising your kids. That may mean becoming a stay at home mom, working only part time, or working from home. That's great, but don't feel like that can't change as time goes by. A few years from now, the kids will all be in school and you find yourself with more time on your hands. It's perfectly fine to switch focus and get back into your career or try something completely new. Things change and evolve. You change and evolve. Your purpose may evolve as well and that's perfectly normal and how it should be.

That's why it's a good idea to occasionally take some time and think about what's important to you and make sure you're still living a purpose driven life based on your current values and ideas. It's ok to change and adjust if things no longer feel like a good fit. While it's something you can do "on the fly" as you move through your days and weeks, it can also be helpful to stop every few months and take time to really think about this.

We are creatures of habit and will often stick to a plan, an idea, or a routine because that's how we've always done it, or out of a desire to tough it out. While that's admirable and there's certainly a time and place for this, it's also good to take some time to reflect and second guess what you're doing.

You want to live your life intentionally and with purpose. That means you should always second guess yourself and make sure you're doing is a good fit and the best way to live purposefully. If it is, great… carry on. If it isn't, make some changes until what you do aligns with your purposes.

## Day 29 - What Do You Want To Be Remembered For?

Here's an interesting question for you. What do you want to be remembered for when you're gone? Since our life on this beautiful earth is limited, it's only natural that we want to leave some sort of legacy. What's yours going to be? What do you want to be remembered for?

Living a purpose driven life makes this a lot easier. You know what you want to accomplish and what impact you want to have on your family, your loved ones, your friends, your community, and the world at large. If that sounds a little overwhelming right now, don't let it intimidate you. You'll get there. Living with purpose starts small for most of us and grows exponentially as we notice the effect we can have on those around us when we start to live intentionally and with an open heart.

Even small changes and accomplishments are nothing to laugh at or dismiss. Raising your children well is an amazing feat and a wonderful legacy to leave behind in the world. Or maybe you will be remembered for the small community garden you started that will long outlive you and show others how tasty and rewarding it can be to grow carrots and tomatoes.
As you start to live with more purpose, you may get to a point where you're wondering what else you can do. You may be asking yourself how you can help people around you and how you can make the world a better place. Asking yourself what you want to be remembered for and what your legacy will be is a great way to figure that out.

Here's a little exercise you can do today. Get out a piece of paper and write down what you would like your eulogy to be. It will condense what you want to be remembered for and what values are important to you. Set it aside for a little while, then come back and read it. As you do so, compare it to the life you're leading right now. What do you need to change? What do you need to work on to make sure your life aligns with the eulogy you wrote for yourself? That's your game plan. It may take a while and it may change over time, and that's ok.

What's important is that we live our short lives with purpose and make the most of the years we're given on this earth. Remind yourself of this and live a life full of things that you'll be proud to be remembered for.

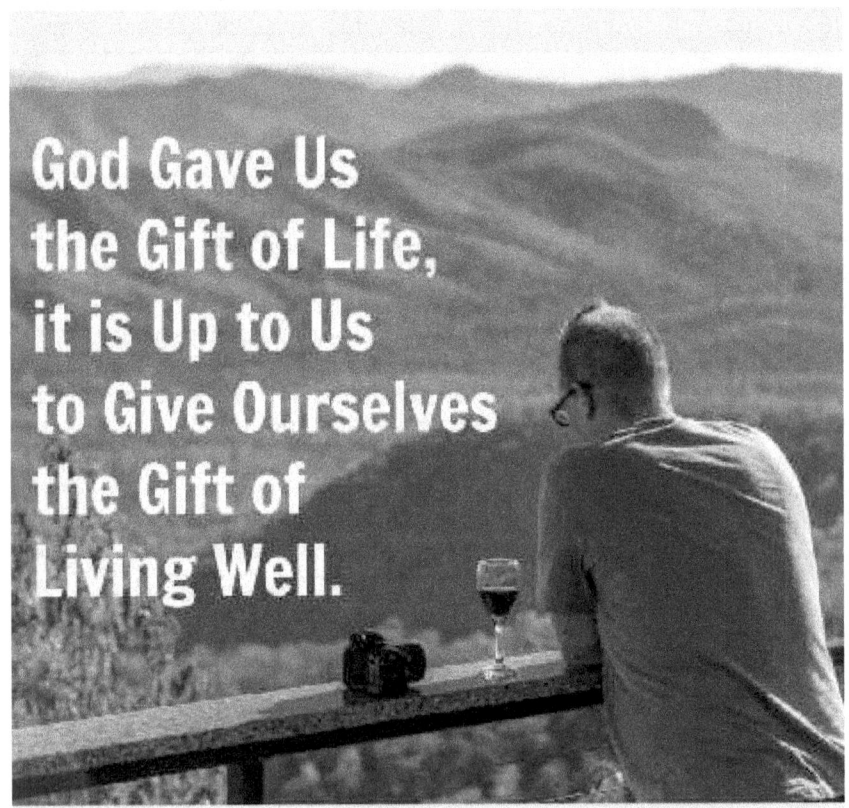

God Gave Us the Gift of Life, it is Up to Us to Give Ourselves the Gift of Living Well.

*Voltaire*

## Day 30 - Wrap Up And Where To Go From Here

It's hard to believe, but we've come to the end of our 30 Day Living With Purpose Challenge. Time flies when you're having fun, doesn't it? I hope you've enjoyed our little journey towards living a more intentional and purpose-driven life as much as I have. More importantly, I hope the daily blog posts have inspired some serious thought and discussion.

Here's what we covered over the past 30 Days
1. Welcome And What Does It Mean To Live With Purpose
2. Why It's Important To Find Your Purpose
3. What Is Your Purpose?
4. The Connection Between Purpose and Happiness
5. Why What You Do For A Living Matters
6. How To Find Your Calling
7. Your Purpose Doesn't Have To Be Huge To Make A Difference
8. Small Things You Can Start Doing Right Now To Make A Difference
9. Do You Know What's Sucking Up Your Time
10. Going From Existing To Truly Living Life
11. Let's Talk About TV And The Likes
12. How Much Time Are You Spending On Facebook
13. Embrace Your Hobbies And Interests
14. Never Stop Learning
15. The Big Benefits Of Traveling The World
16. Creating Purposeful And Meaningful Relationships
17. When You Have A Purpose, You're Taking Action And Aren't Afraid Of Failure
18. Living With Purpose Is Good For Your Spiritual Health
19. Guess What? Money And "Stuff" Doesn't Make You Happy
20. Living With Purpose Makes You A Kinder Person
21. When You Live With Purpose, You Don't Have Time To Worry
22. When You Live A Purpose Driven Life, Your Values Are Clear
23. You Realize The World Doesn't Revolve Around You
24. Aligning Yourself With Your Purpose Through Mediation And Prayer
25. Avoid Temptations And Wrong Paths Along The Way
26. Living With Purpose Is About Serving Your Community
27. Your Loved Ones Will Benefit From A Purpose Driven Life
28. Your Purpose May Evolve And Change As You Do… And That's Ok
29. What Do You Want To Be Remembered For?

The next question is of course where you go from here. Frankly, it's up to you. We've given you a lot of ideas, tools, and suggestions to craft a more purposeful life for yourself and your loved ones. What you do with that information is up to you. We hope you've been following along, doing a lot of thinking, and have started to implement. We encourage you to continue on this journey. Keep bringing more meaning and purpose into your life. Keep reading, keep learning, and keep on making progress.

## About The Authors:

Lynn and Richard help clients clarify their passion and talents in order to develop unique strategies that paint dreams, excite eyeballs, and market messages. They help everyday people accomplish goals by creating an action plan that discovers and connects the missing pieces of a client's success puzzle.

Together, they present a unique team-approach with each client, working side-by-side; utilizing their life-long skills and diverse expertise as artists, authors, publishers, & educational consultants.

Teaching by example, they focus on proven systems, research and development, trends & technology, key domain portfolio acquisitions, video production, self-publishing, along with managing a variety of premium keyword websites on behalf of their company, RIVO Inc – RIVO Marketing.

Their life-long mission is to continually uncover brand new ideas, strategies, products, and services, networking useful solutions for their clients, online & offline entrepreneurs, small business owners, writers, artists, models, teachers, and marketing professionals.

Feel free to contact them if you have questions or would like to tap into their talents and expertise. They'd appreciate your feedback and hearing about your success story.

Richard & Lynn Voigt
Educational Consultants

RIVO Inc. – RIVO Books
13720 Keefe Avenue
Brookfield, WI 53005
Educational Consultants

Website: www.RIVObooks.com
Email: support@RIVOinc.com

# www.RIVO BOOKS.com

### Richard & Lynn Voigt

**Develop Dreams - Excite Eyeballs - Market Messages**

## Look For More RIVO Book Titles Available On Amazon

**DOODLING FOR ADULTS**
Much More Than Just Another Coloring Book

**DOODLE DESIGNS - Vol. 1**
**DOODLE DESIGNS - Vol. 2**

**SECOND OF FIVE** - Lynn's Memoir - Episode #1
My Early Years - From Birth To High School

**TWO BECOME ONE** - Lynn's Memoir - Episode #2
Dating, College, Teaching & Marriage

**SECOND OF FIVE AGAIN** - Lynn's Memoir - Episode #3
Raising 3 Children & A Husband - COMING SOON!

**BABY NAMES - 2014 Edition**
32,250 Baby Names with Origins & Meanings PLUS
Top 100 Names & 2,000 Most Popular Names

**GARDEN CONVERSATIONS**
901 Garden Poems, Quotations, & Classic Words Of Wisdom

**WI GARDEN - LET'S GET DIRTY**
Promoting Tips, Tools & Techniques That Inspire
Gardeners Around The World

**SEARCHING FOR SOUL**
Simple Exercises That Can Help Clarify
The Meaning Of Life

**QUOTATIONS ABOUT SOUL**
500 Inspirational & Motivational Quotations
About Soul

**The GOLDEN VAULT OF QUOTATIONS**
Words Of Wisdom From The Greatest Minds & Leaders

**HEADLINE STARTERS**
175,000 Words The Paint Dreams, Sell Ideas
& Market Messages

**MORE THAN WORDS**
5000+ Market Phrases That Sell

**HYPNOTIC PHRASING**
WARNING - This Book Teaches You How To Grab Eyeballs

**ACTION HEADLINES That Drive Emotions Vol. 1**
5,000 Unique Phrases For Marketing Ideas
**ACTION HEADLINES That Drive Emotions Vol. 2**
5,000 Unique Phrases For Marketing Ideas
**ACTION HEADLINES That Drive Emotions Vol. 3**
5,000 Unique Phrases For Marketing Ideas
**ACTION HEADLINES That Drive Emotions Vol. 4**
5,000 Unique Phrases For Marketing Ideas
**ACTION HEADLINES That Drive Emotions Vol. 5**
5,000 Unique Phrases For Marketing Ideas
**ACTION HEADLINES That Drive Emotions Vol. 6**
5,000 Unique Phrases For Marketing Ideas

**POWER PHRASES (Complete Series Vol. 1-10)**
5,000 Power Phases That Trigger Greater Profits

**FUNNY HEADLINES Vol.1**
**FUNNY HEADLINES Vol.1**
3,500 Outrageous Silly Brain Toots

**MONEY WORDS**
Powerful Phrases That Million Dollar Copywriters Use
To Make Piles Of Cash On Demand

**CURIOUS WORDS**
15,800 Words That Expand Minds & Change Lives

**CLICHE BIBLE**
8,400 Cliches For Sports Fanatics & Lovers
Of Popular Expressions

**IDIOMS - IDIOMS - IDIOMS**
6,450 Popular Expressions That Put Words In My Mouth

**INSPIRING THOUGHTS**
That Inspire Happiness, Success & A Clearer
Understanding Of Life

**MARKETING EYEBALLS**
100 Ideas Than Can Add Unlimited Subscribers

**MY LIFE MATTERS**
Recording A Meaningful & Fulfilling Life

**MY GRATITUDE JOURNAL**
Loving Relationships, Health, Financial Independence
& So Much More

**THE BEAUTY OF GRATITUDE**
Attracting More Joy & Happiness Into Your Life

**The AMAZING GRATITUDE JOURNAL**
For Girls Who Love Having Fun

**The GRATITUDE JOURNAL**
For Men On A Success-Oriented Mission

**GRATITUDE JOURNEY**
Experience The Magic Of Keeping A Gratitude Journal

**The MAGIC INSIDE A GRATITUDE JOURNAL**
Experience The Endless Gifts Of Life

**The LIGHTHOUSE BUCKET LIST**
Recording Great Memories For Your Lighthouse Visits

**The GARDEN GRATITUDE JOURNAL**
Recording Precous Moments In Your Garden

**MY SECRET DIARY** - Love, Hope & Dreams

**MY DARKEST THOUGHTS**
Confronting Fear, Anxiety & Worry To Live Happier

**DAILY RANTS**
Turning Outrage Into A Power Tool For Change

**THE MAGIC WISH LIST**
Every Miracle Begins With Passion & Action

**MY DREAM JOURNAL**
Recording Dream Visions Before They Disappear

**MY SKETCHBOOK**
Exploring Creative Thoughts & Ideas

**The DOODLE DUMPSTER**
A Creative Playground For Your Mind

**LET'S GET DIRTY**
Playing In The Garden Soil

**MY LITTLE BLACK BOOK**
Keeping Track Of Important Contacts Offline

www.ingramcontent.com/pod-product-compliance
Lightning Source LLC
Chambersburg PA
CBHW061312040426
42444CB00010B/2602